DISCARD

ancient greeks

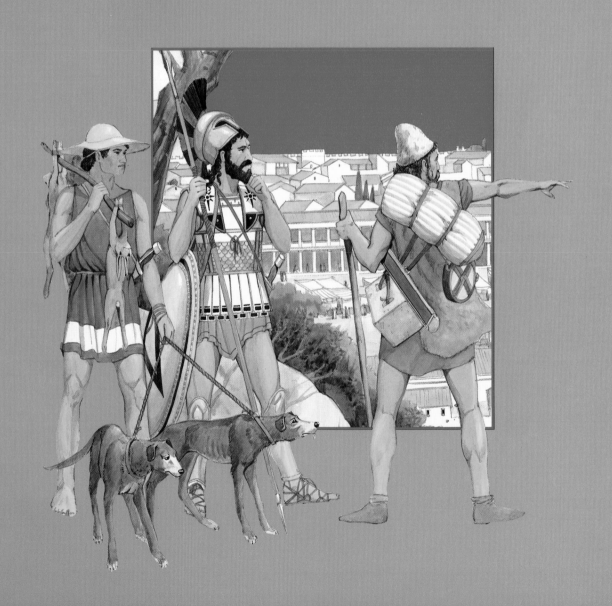

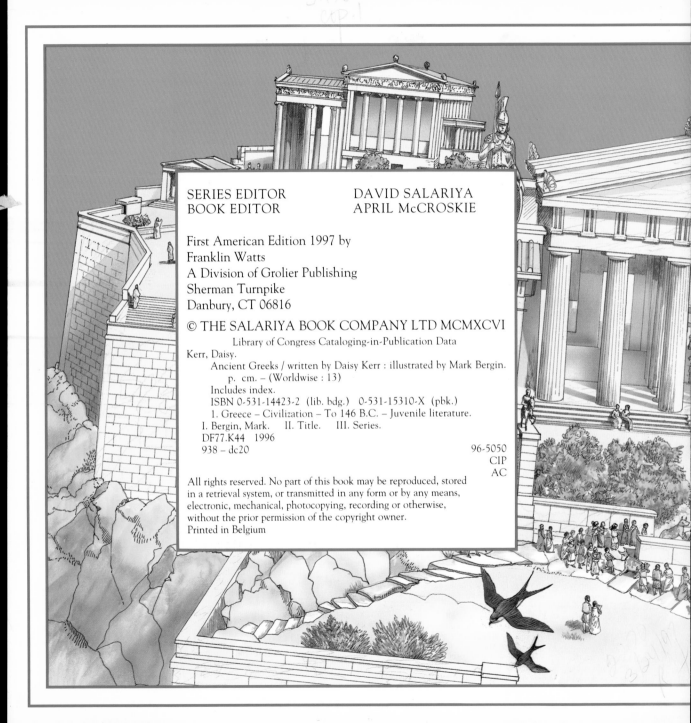

| SERIES EDITOR | DAVID SALARIYA |
| BOOK EDITOR | APRIL McCROSKIE |

First American Edition 1997 by
Franklin Watts
A Division of Grolier Publishing
Sherman Turnpike
Danbury, CT 06816

Library of Congress Cataloging-in-Publication Data
Kerr, Daisy.
  Ancient Greeks / written by Daisy Kerr : illustrated by Mark Bergin.
    p. cm. – (Worldwise : 13)
  Includes index.
  ISBN 0-531-14423-2 (lib. bdg.) 0-531-15310-X (pbk.)
  1. Greece – Civilization – To 146 B.C. – Juvenile literature.
  I. Bergin, Mark.   II. Title.   III. Series.
  DF77.K44 1996
  938 – dc20   96-5050
                                                                   CIP
                                                                    AC

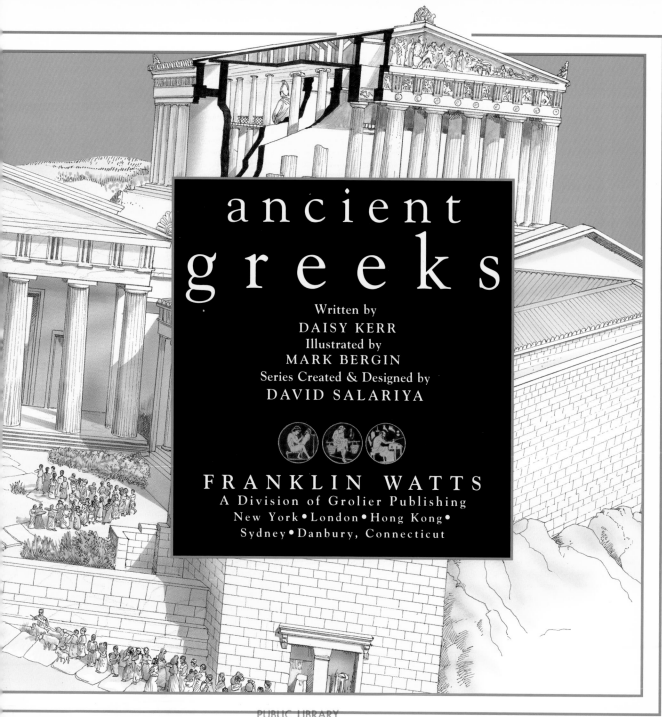

ancient
greeks

Written by
DAISY KERR

Illustrated by
MARK BERGIN

Series Created & Designed by
DAVID SALARIYA

FRANKLIN WATTS
A Division of Grolier Publishing
New York•London•Hong Kong•
Sydney•Danbury, Connecticut

CONTENTS

j938
Cop. 1
9/97

22.70
3/24/97

The ancient Greeks lived over 2,500 years ago.

Greek civilization flourished from around 800-350 B.C. Greek armies were brave and strong. Scholars were clever, craftworkers and artists were skillful, and merchants were rich.

Philip of Macedon conquered Greek lands in 338 B.C., but Greek civilization did not disappear completely. We still admire many Greek buildings and works of art. We still use some Greek words. And we still rely on many Greek inventions and discoveries today.

The Greek

homeland was present-day Greece. But the "Greek world" stretched all around the Mediterranean Sea, from southern Europe to the north of Africa. Many Greek people lived in Cyprus and Turkey, and on islands off the Greek and Turkish coasts. Merchants sailed between these settlements. The Greeks built new towns in southern Italy and on the shores of the Black Sea.

MACEDON

Athens

GREECE

Sparta

MEDITERRANEAN SEA

CRETE

Area in red shows the Greek world.

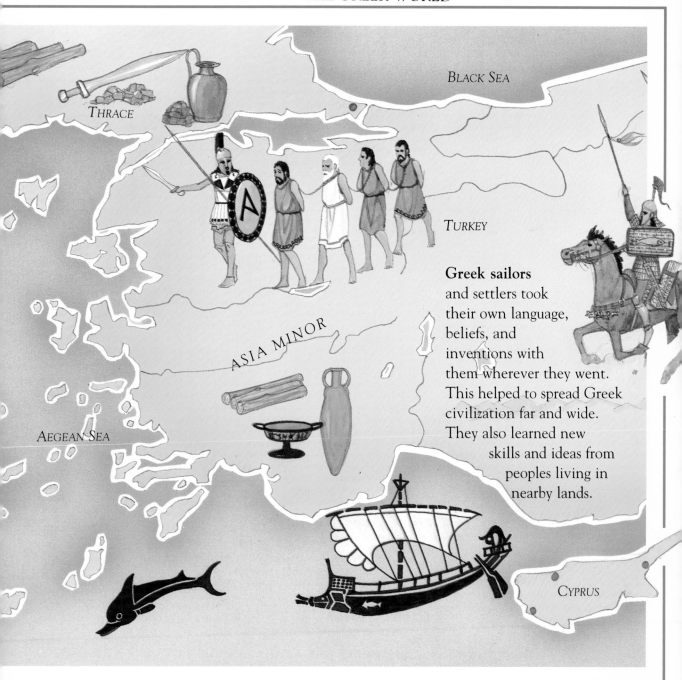

BLACK SEA

THRACE

TURKEY

ASIA MINOR

AEGEAN SEA

Greek sailors and settlers took their own language, beliefs, and inventions with them wherever they went. This helped to spread Greek civilization far and wide. They also learned new skills and ideas from peoples living in nearby lands.

CYPRUS

At harvest time, the whole family worked hard to collect ripe olives and press them to make oil.

The land of ancient Greece was very beautiful, with mountains, forests, cliffs, and streams. But the soil was thin and stony. Only a few crops such as olives, grapes, and grain would grow there.

Olive trees

Picking olives

Olive press

Olive oil

10

And only a few goats and tough mountain sheep could survive. The climate was harsh. Summers were very hot and sunny, but winters could be bitterly cold.

Greek farmhouses were made of mud walls, with roofs of clay tiles. Windows had strong wooden shutters to keep out robbers.

Courtyard

Farmhouse

Mountain sheep

Rough mountain road

11

Coins from Greek city-states. Each city's coin had a different design.

Slaves captured in wars were bought and sold in the agora (marketplace).

Athenian citizens could go to the assembly to make speeches and pass new laws. Citizens could be members of a jury in the lawcourts and help run the army.

Huge ivory statue of the goddess Athena. She protected the city of Athens.

The Greek world was divided up into many city-states. Each had a town, or a city, plus farm land all around. Athens was the biggest and most powerful city-state. It had a rich empire in foreign lands.

Ostraka

The Parthenon (built 447-432 B.C.) was a temple dedicated to the goddess Athena.

Citizens voted by casting clay ballots or ostraka into a big clay jar.

Ballot

Citizen soldiers kept guard outside the city gates and the city walls.

Pericles (top) was the most famous ruler of Athens. He lived around 500-429 B.C. Socrates (bottom) was a famous Greek philosopher. He lived 470-399 B.C. He taught his students to think and ask questions about life.

Early city-states were ruled by kings. Around 600 B.C., they were replaced by powerful, rich men. After about 500 B.C., many city-states became democracies. All adult males had the right to take part in government.

Silver coin made in Athens, decorated with an olive branch and Athena's owl.

Many non-Greek peoples also lived in Greek cities. Foreigners, women, and children did not have citizens' rights.

Farmers brought fruit, oil and grain into the city on mules. In wartime, enemy armies surrounded the city and cut off food supplies.

In 482 B.C., the Athenians found silver close to the city. They sent criminals and slaves to dig deep mines. Conditions in the mines were terrible, but the city of Athens grew wealthy.

Athens had temples, theaters, sports arenas, schools, government offices, stores, and taverns.

In summertime, Greek cities were full of flies, because there were no sewers.

Houses in Greek cities were packed tightly together. Poor citizens lived in simple, single-story homes.

In 450 B.C., about 250,000 people lived in the city of Athens.

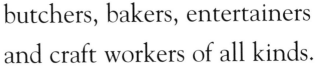

In early Greek times, most people lived and worked in the countryside. But after around 700 B.C., they started to move to the cities. They found they could make a better living there, as shopkeepers, butchers, bakers, entertainers and craft workers of all kinds.

Wealthier citizens lived in well-planned homes, with rooms for preparing and cooking food and for entertaining guests.

The family said prayers at the altar every day.

Greek homes were often built around a courtyard, which let in sunlight and fresh air. They were protected from the dirt and bustle of city streets by strong gates and thick walls.

Bedroom

Upstairs, there were private rooms where women and their slaves worked and relaxed, away from male company.

Stool

Couch

Table

Meals were cooked over an open fire on a hearth made of large stones. Food was stored in large, rat-proof clay jars, called amphorae.

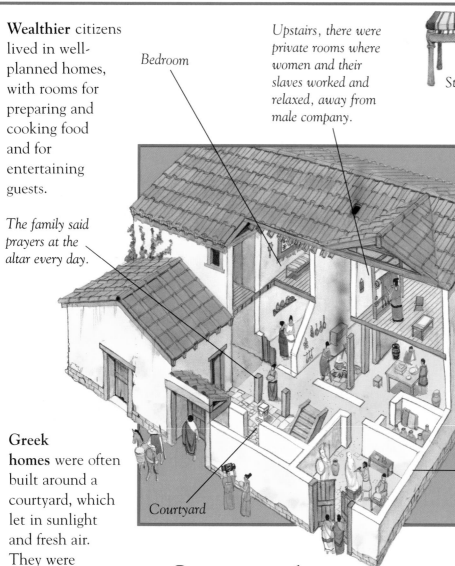

Courtyard

Craftsmen worked at home. Visitors came to their work rooms to admire and buy craft goods.

Cities were busy, noisy, crowded, and they often smelled bad. Overcrowding led to quarrels, riots, food shortages, and disease.

There were many

well-trained craftworkers living in Greek cities – weavers, potters, painters, sculptors, goldsmiths, and leather workers. Some made solid, durable goods, like shoes and cooking pots, for ordinary people to use. Others produced beautiful masterpieces that only rich people could afford.

The simplest craft goods were made by the poorer women. They spun thread and wove cloth to make rough cloaks, rugs, and blankets to keep their families warm.

Potters made jugs, bowls, vases, and cups from clay, which was fired and then painted with beautiful designs.

Leather workers made sandals, soldiers' boots, and workers' aprons from ox hide and goat skin.

Sculptors carved statues, tombstones, and fancy columns for temples out of fine white marble stone.

—Kiln

Pottery was fired in a red-hot kiln. When it cooled, it was painted with pictures of gods, heroes, or scenes from everyday life.

Upright loom

Greek men and women wore loose, simple, and elegant clothes.

Engraved gemstone

Greek jewelers liked to engrave (carve) amazingly detailed pictures onto precious gemstones.

Women spun fine thread from the wool of sheep, then wove it into cloth on tall upright looms.

Necklace

Chiton

Bracelet

The best stone carvers and sculptors moved from city to city. They worked on temples, palaces, and other fine buildings.

Peplos

Himation

Greek goldsmiths created fabulous jewelry like this gold bracelet, decorated with animal heads, and this necklace of silver beads.

Women wore a floor-length tunic, called a peplos. Other garments were a knee-length tunic called a chiton and a cloak called a himation.

Sandals and boots, suitable for Greece's hot, dry weather

Athens

Macedon

Syracuse

Syracuse
(reverse of coin)

Corinth

Aegina

Coins were invented in Lydia (in present-day Turkey) around 690 B.C. They were soon used all over Greece. Each city made its own out of silver or gold.

Traders weighed coins before accepting them to make sure they were real.

Buyers and sellers haggled over prices. Everyone wanted to find a bargain.

Farmers brought eggs and chickens to sell. There was no room in the city to grow food.

The marketplace was the social center of each Greek city. Citizens went there every day to buy food. They also went to the market to meet their friends to discuss local politics and the latest news.

In big towns, people could buy "take-out" foods from market stalls.

Men or slaves usually did all the shopping. Servants and slaves carried water from street fountains. "Respectable" women stayed at home.

Fishermen carried fresh fish and seafood from the harbor to the market.

Few Greek people could afford to eat these favorite foods every day:
1. fish 2. squid
3. shellfish 4. fresh herbs 5. olives
6. figs 7. bread
8. chicken
9. cheese 10. ham

City-states grew rich by taxing trade. So they encouraged trade by building new markets, with rooms nearby where bankers and money changers could work.

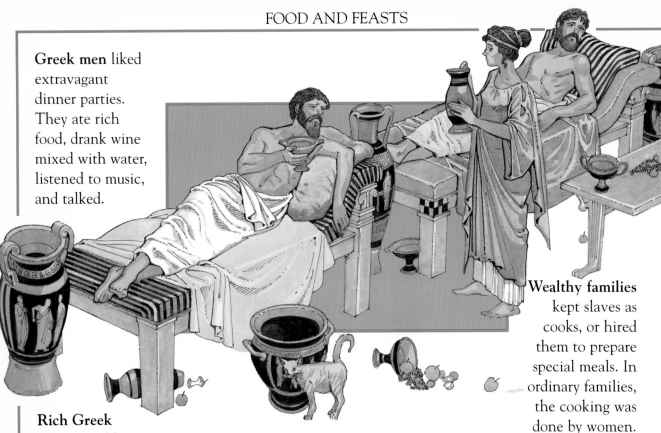

Greek men liked extravagant dinner parties. They ate rich food, drank wine mixed with water, listened to music, and talked.

Wealthy families kept slaves as cooks, or hired them to prepare special meals. In ordinary families, the cooking was done by women.

Rich Greek people could afford beautifully decorated cups and plates.

This cup, decorated with a ram's head, was for drinking water and wine.

Greek families ate foods like bread, beans, olives, grapes, and figs. In summer, everyone ate fresh vegetables and herbs. In winter, they ate foods harvested in autumn and carefully stored, such as apples, chestnuts, lentils, and goat cheese.

Favorite entertainments were plays, music, and dancing. Plays were staged in open-air theaters and performed by actors in masks and elaborate costumes. A performance might last all day. Many plays were written to criticize the government.

Theaters were built with sloping rows of seats in a half-circle shape.

Poor people were given money by the citizens to pay for cheap seats.

The largest Greek theater, at Epidaurus, could seat around 14,000 people.

Greek actors were well trained. They had stamina and a good memory. Plays included dancing, singing, and mime.

Actors wore comic (happy) or tragic (sad) masks, depending on the part they were playing.

21

Greek boys and girls were educated differently. Rich boys went to school, where they learned reading, writing, dancing, music, and math. Older boys might also study science, philosophy, or law. Exercise was important, too. Boys from ordinary families were trained by their fathers in farming, trading, or craft skills. All Greek girls were educated at home. Rich girls learned how to manage a household and give orders to slaves. Ordinary girls learned cooking, cleaning, weaving, and child care.

The Greeks invented an alphabet – a way of writing using symbols for different sounds. We still use these letters in a modern form.

A	B	Γ	Δ	E	Z	H	Θ	I	K	Λ	M	N	Ξ
A	B	C	D	E	Z	E	Th	I	K	L	M	N	X
O	Π	P	Σ	T	Y	Φ	X	Ψ	Ω				
O	P	R	S	T	U	Ph	Kh	Ps	O				
						F	Ch						

Sappho, a poetess, lived in the 6th century B.C. She was famous for her love poems.

This fragment of Sappho's poetry has survived.

Dancers

Lyre

Girls were trained to dance. Dancing was good exercise and formed an important part of many festivals.

Popular instruments included lyres, flutes, pan pipes, tambourines, and the kithara – an early form of the guitar.

Greek men and women danced to the music of many different instruments.

23

The Acropolis was an ancient fortress built on a high rock in the center of Athens. The Athenians built many fine temples there, to honor their gods and goddesses.

Priestesses, called oracles, claimed to be able to see into the future. They had visions after being drugged by poisonous smoke from burning laurel leaves. The most famous oracle was at Delphi.

Oracle

The Acropolis (high fortress) of Athens

The statue of Athena was about 55 feet high

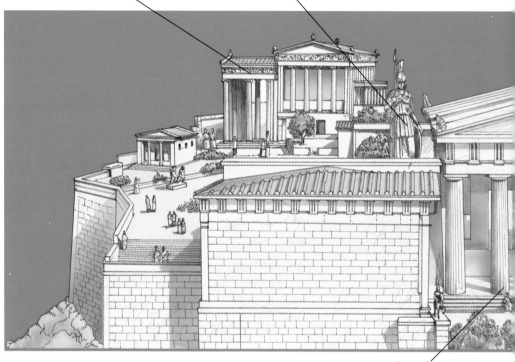

Grand gateway

Ancient Greeks believed in many different gods and goddesses. Some watched over cities and some controlled the crops. Some brought love and wealth, and others caused war, disease, and death.

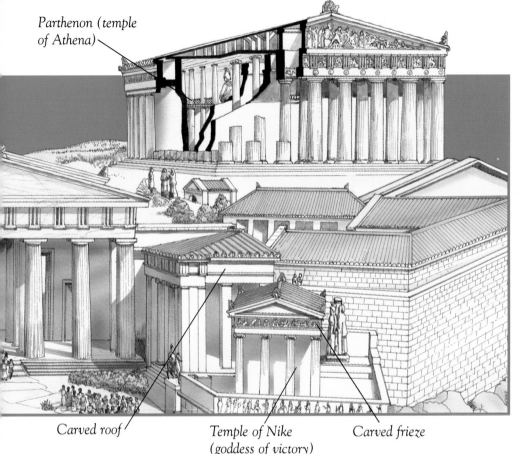

Parthenon (temple of Athena)

Carved roof

Temple of Nike (goddess of victory)

Carved frieze

Temples were built as houses for goddesses and gods. Temples were built of the finest stone and decorated with paintings, carvings, and statues.

Zeus was king of the gods. He ruled the heavens and the earth.

Hera

Artemis

Apollo

The Greeks built magnificent temples for their gods and goddesses, and made offerings to them. They hoped the gods would help them in return.

Hera was queen of heaven and looked after women and children. Apollo was god of the sun. He played the lyre and inspired musicians. His twin sister, Artemis, was the goddess of hunting.

Pythagoras (572-497 B.C.) was a famous Greek mathematician. He started up a community of scholars, in southern Italy, to study math and religion.

Greek astronomers studied the moon and the stars carefully. They named many groups of stars.

Greek geographers invented methods to calculate the distance around the world.

The ancient Greeks were skilled scientists. Greek mathematicians discovered rules about numbers and shapes. Greek inventors designed automatic doors and the first slot machines. And Greek geographers were the first to suggest that the world was round.

Greek medicine was a mixture of science and religion. Greek doctors believed that the gods helped healing. But they also discovered that our surroundings, our food and our state of mind all affect our health.

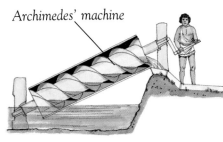

Archimedes' machine

Archimedes (287-212 B.C.) designed a machine to make water flow uphill. The design was used for almost 2,000 years.

Greek "klepsydra" (water clock)

Asclepius was the god of healing. His priests worked as doctors in temples.

Greek doctors were trained to make scientific examinations of their patients. This helped them understand and cure diseases.

Some patients chose faith healing. They stayed overnight in temples. They hoped to be cured by a "visit" from the god in a vision or a dream.

Hospitals were attached to a few big temples. Patients lay on beds in a shaded colonnade. They made offerings to the gods at an altar in the center of the courtyard.

Patients who had been cured at a temple left offerings in the shape of the part of their body that had been healed.

Blood letting

The Greeks believed that our bodies contain balanced amounts of four liquids. If this was disturbed, blood letting (removing blood) put the balance right again.

Greek medical instruments – hooks, spatulas, probes, and tongs, plus a mortar and pestle, used to grind herbs to make medicines.

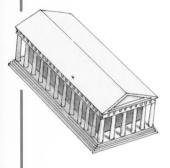

Temples were designed with rows of columns supporting a massive roof. They were decorated with many fine carvings.

This frieze shows a battle between a man and a monster called a satyr.

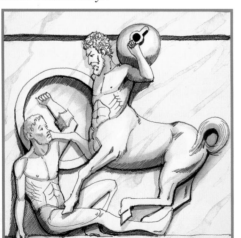

Religious festivals played an important part in many Greek cities. They were held to honor all the different gods or goddesses. Sometimes festivals were held in memory of ancient local heroes, as well. Nobody worked on festival days. Instead, they said prayers at the temples or danced in processions through the streets, playing music. People brought offerings, such as animals wearing beautiful flower garlands, to give to the gods and goddesses.

A beautiful frieze, carved in stone, was fixed around the top of the Parthenon building, about 40 feet above the ground. It shows a festival procession walking from the center of the city of Athens to the altar of the goddess Athena, which stood in front of the Parthenon.

Olympia was an ancient holy site. Games were first held there in 776 B.C., in honor of the god Zeus.

Guest house and sports practice ground

Many splendid buildings were built for visitors to stay in during the Olympic Games.

Athlete with helmet and shield

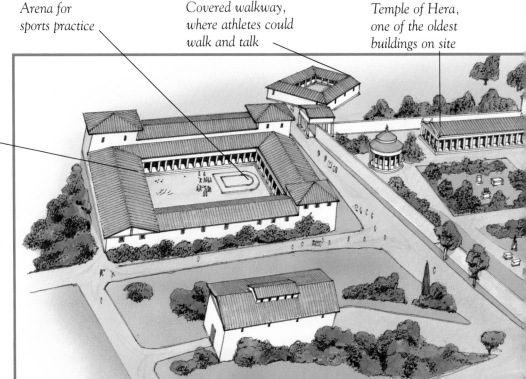

Arena for sports practice

Covered walkway, where athletes could walk and talk

Temple of Hera, one of the oldest buildings on site

Sports were important to the Greeks. They were fun and provided good training for war. Soldiers built up their strength by running in armor, throwing spears, wrestling, and boxing. These sports were useful when it came to fighting real enemies.

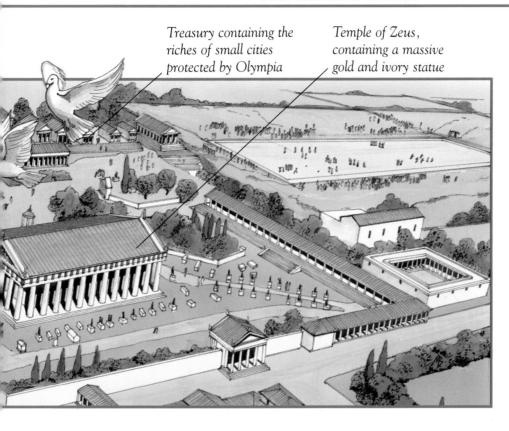

Treasury containing the riches of small cities protected by Olympia

Temple of Zeus, containing a massive gold and ivory statue

The stadium was almost 650 feet long and 100 feet wide. The race track was covered with white sand and the starting line was made of stone. Referees kept order with big sticks.

Female athlete

The Olympic Games were held for five days, every four years. Victorious sportsmen won fame and fortune. They were given a crown of leaves and ribbons, and prizes of olive oil, fine fabrics, and pottery. Poems were written to praise them.

A separate sports festival, to honor the goddess Hera, was organized for women.

Coins showing riding; winner's crown of leaves; chariot racing.

Soldiers fighting in a phalanx formation

Greek soldiers fought with sharp iron swords, long, bronze-tipped spears and wooden shields. Weapons, helmets and armor were passed on proudly from father to son.

Greek city-states were often at war. They fought against one another, and they also fought together as friends against enemies from abroad. All men over 18 were expected to join the army. In Athens, young men had to spend two years training.

Greek soldiers fought mostly on foot. In battle, they advanced side by side in a "phalanx" formation. This presented a wall of shields to the enemy. The soldiers of one phalanx threw their spears at another, hoping to make the enemy run away.

Some city-states had professional soldiers, recruited from nearby lands. They fought with sling shots (strips of fabric for hurling stones) or with bows and arrows.

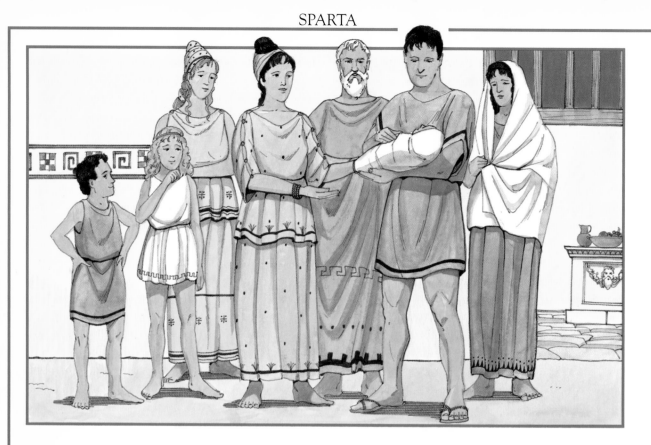

Each baby was examined by Spartan elders. If it was weak or sickly, it would not be allowed to live. Spartan women had to train hard and keep fit so they would have healthy babies.

Sparta was a city-state in southern Greece. It was not a democracy like Athens. Instead, it was ruled by two kings and a council of elders. Only a few Spartan citizens were free. The rest were called helots and were treated like slaves. They were guarded closely, in case they tried to riot or run away. The helots hated the citizens, the elders, and the kings. Spartan citizens lived very simply, so they would always be ready for war. Rich foods, warm clothes, and comfortable homes were forbidden.

By age 7, Spartan boys were taken away to be trained by the state.

Spartan soldiers stood guard over the helots working in the field in case they ran away.

Spartan wedding. Husbands spent most of their time away in the army.

Spartan citizens did not trade. Only non-citizens could work as merchants.

Spartan women athletes trained hard.

Spartan women were trained to take part in games, so they would be fit and strong. Other Greeks were shocked by their short tunics.

Many important wars

were fought at sea. In a sea battle, enemy warships tried to ram and sink one another.

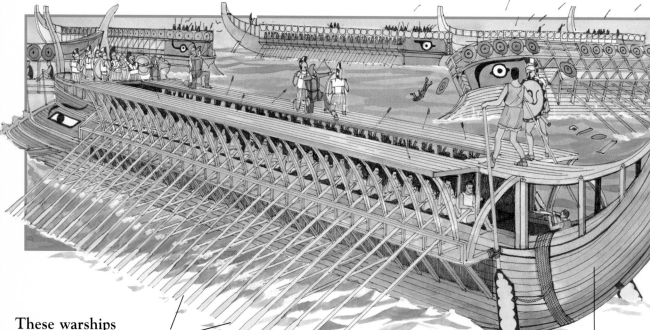

Oars

Paddle

Stern

These warships were called triremes. They were rowed by 170 people, who kept time to the music of a flute. Triremes were steered by two huge paddles at the stern.

The Persians (from present-day Iran) were the Greeks' most powerful enemy. Persian soldiers and sailors invaded Greece in 490 B.C. and again in 480 B.C.

In 480 B.C., the Athenian navy, led by General Themistocles, destroyed Persian ships at the Battle of Salamis. This battle defeated the Persian invasion.

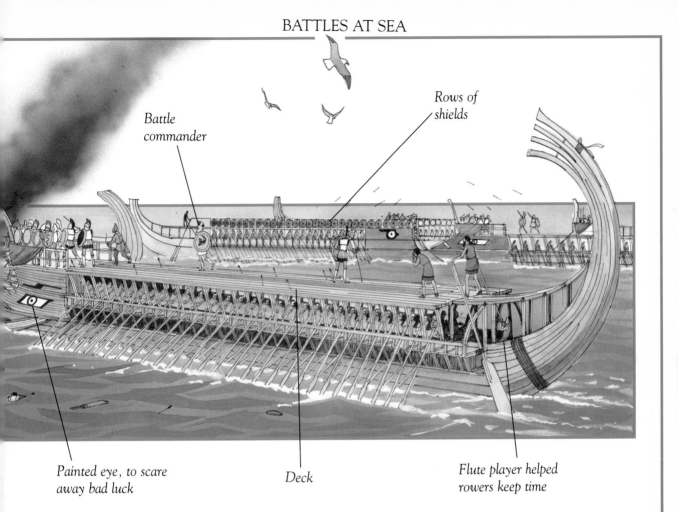

Battle
commander

Rows of
shields

Painted eye, to scare
away bad luck

Deck

Flute player helped
rowers keep time

If an attacking ship failed to sink its enemy, it sailed as close as possible to it, so that the decks were side by side. Then soldiers would leap on board and slaughter the passengers and crew. Invading armies relied on sea transport for carrying soldiers, weapons, and food.

USEFUL WORDS

Agora Market-place.

Amphora Storage jar made of clay.

Astronomers People who study the sun, moon and stars.

Ballot Clay token used to vote.

Chiton Knee-length tunic.

Colonnade Covered walkway; a roof supported on columns.

Democracy A government where the people rule.

Empire Lands ruled by another, stronger country.

Engrave To carve a design on a hard, smooth surface.

Frieze Carved border fixed to a wall.

Helots Non-citizens who lived in Sparta. They were treated like slaves.

Himation Long cloak usually made of wool.

Mortar and pestle Heavy bowl and stick, used to crush and grind herbs to make medicines.

Oracle Priestess who claimed to be able to see into the future.

Ostraka Fragment of pottery on which Athenian citizens wrote the names of people they wanted to ban from their city.

Peplos Long tunic, worn by women.

Phalanx Row of foot-soldiers standing with their shields. Used in battle.

Philosophy The study of ideas.

Symposium Dinner party, for men only.

Trireme A fast Greek warship, with three rows of oars.

INDEX